*Breathe God: A 7 Day Journey to Experience God* is a published work of Tiffany C. Fuller. No part of this publication may be reproduced in whole or in part by any resources such as electronic, mechanical, photocopy, recording, or any other manner without written permission from Tiffany C. Fuller.

Editor, Formatter, & Publisher:
J & I Publishing LLC

Address all inquiries to email:
tiff101@hotmail.com

Copyright © 2021 Tiffany C. Fuller

All rights reserved.

ISBN: 978-1-7372056-1-6

# Breathe God

A 7 Day Journey to Experience God

Tiffany C. Fuller

# TABLE OF CONTENTS

DEDICATION ......................... 1

Introduction ......................... 2-5

Opening Prayer ...................... 6-7

Day 1 .................................... 8-17

Day 2 .................................... 18-29

Day 3 .................................... 30-41

Day 4 .................................... 42-53

Day 5 .................................... 54-65

| | |
|---|---|
| Day 6 | 66-77 |
| Day 7 | 78-87 |
| Poem | 88 |
| Website | 89 |

# DEDICATION

This devotional/journal is dedicated to my late grandma Mary L. Fuller. My grandma was loving, caring, and full of wisdom.

# Introduction

So, why did I write this devotional you might ask? Why did I decide to create one? Well thanks for asking, and let me tell you. One day I was listening to a prayer and it suggested that the listener inhale, exhale, and relax. And these words came to me:

Inhale God's love,
exhale hate

Inhale God's peace,
exhale all anxiety

Inhale God's joy,
exhale unhappiness

Inhale God's forgiveness,
exhale past mistakes

Inhale God's will,
exhale all doubts,
worry and fears

These words came to me so easily at 12:45 a.m. on that March morning in 2018 that I was inspired to create this journal, so that I can share with the world what God shared with me. I pray that you enjoy these next seven days of your life and that you experience God like never before.

For the next seven days, I would like for you to journal your thoughts after each reading. I also ask that while you are reading the entry for the day that you go to a secluded place, so that you can hear from God away from distractions.

~Tiffany Fuller

# Opening Prayer

Dear Father God,

Thank you for allowing us to see another day. Father God, thank you for your grace, love, kindness, and forgiveness. Father, I pray that the person who is going to go through this 7 day journey will be different from the person that they are today. I pray that their lives are changed from this day forward. Lord, I ask you that if this person feels lost or confused that you show them the way.

In Jesus' name,

Amen.

# Day 1

Go to a quiet place where there are no distractions. Read the words below; take a deep breathe; inhale then exhale. Read the poem three times in a row, breathe slowly.

Inhale God's love,
exhale hate

Inhale God's peace,
exhale all anxiety

Inhale God's joy,
exhale unhappiness

Inhale God's forgiveness,
exhale past mistakes

Inhale God's will,
exhale all doubts,
worry and fears

# Recommended Scripture Reading:

*Psalms 139*

Recommended Worship Song:

*Breathe into Me Oh Lord*

by Fred Hammond

# How do you feel? Journal your thoughts below.

_____

_____

_____

_____

_____

# Day 2

## Inhale God's Love, Exhale Hate

Go to a place where there are no distractions and where no one can bother you. Take a deep breath, feels good, doesn't it?

Take another deep breath, and while inhaling think about the love of God our Father, think about how He loves us. Now exhale, exhale anything that is not like God. Exhale the hate in your heart; exhale the things that are not of God. There's so much hate in this world. People can hate you for the color of your skin, your political affiliation, or even when you don't agree with their way of thinking. Hate can affect every area of your life. God loves us, Jesus commands us that we love our neighbors as ourselves; so if you have hatred in your heart towards anyone take it to God; He will help you overcome it.

# Recommended Scripture Readings:

*1 John 4:7*

*1 John 4:19*

*John 15:12*

*Psalm 86:15*

*Proverbs 10:12*

# Recommend Worship Song:

## *One Thing Remains* by Jesus Culture

# How do you feel? Journal your thoughts below.

_____

_____

_____

_____

_____

# Day 3

## Inhale God's Peace, Exhale All Anxiety

We all want peace in our lives; everything is so fast paced in our society nowadays. People rarely get a chance to just breathe.

Today, find some time to spend with God. During this time, take a deep breath and take in the peace of God and exhale all of your anxiety.

Just let go and let God in. God is bigger than our problems. Whatever you are anxious about, talk to our Heavenly Father about it. He is waiting to hear from you.

# Recommended Scripture Readings:

*Psalms 4:8*

*Psalms 34:4*

*John 14:27*

*Isaiah 26:3*

*Numbers 6: 24-26*

… Recommended Worship Song:

*Surrender* by Hillsong

# How do you feel? Journal your thoughts below.

_____

_____

_____

_____

_____

# Day 4.

Inhale God's Joy
Exhale Unhappiness

When a child wakes up in the morning, they usually wake up with a smile on their face; they are so happy and joyful. Children are always filled with so much joy; they do not have a care in the world, because they know that someone will make sure they are ok. So many things happen in life. Life rarely goes the way we want. We lose people to death, we lose jobs, and we lose family and friends due to broken relationships.

While we may lose people and things, remember that life is not happening without God. Life is happening with God. God gives us joy and strength to go through whatever life throws at us.

You should not rest in unhappiness for too long, because the joy of the Lord is your strength and you can make it.

# Recommended Scripture Readings:

*Nehemiah 8:10*

*Proverbs 17:22*

*Romans 15:13*

*Isaiah 41:10*

*Psalm 32:10*

Recommend Worship Song:

*Joy* by Vashawn Mitchell

# How do you feel? Journal your thoughts below.

_____

_____

_____

_____

_____

# Day 5

Inhale God's Forgiveness,

Exhale Past Mistakes

To forgive is to set an act aside, canceling it, as if it had never happened. Forgiveness is an act of love, mercy, and grace. When Jesus died on the cross for our sins, our slate was wiped clean. Yet some of us are still holding on to past sins that our Heavenly Father has already forgiven. We may hold on to the hurt of choices we made in the past. But we must move forward. God forgives us. God sent His only son to die for us. Mistakes are a part of our lives.

We are not a perfect people, but we are saved by grace. Pray to our Heavenly Father and ask for forgiveness. Pour your heart out to Him.

Recommended Scripture Readings:

*Ephesians 4:32*

*Psalms 86:15*

*Mark 11:25*

*Romans 8:37-39*

*Isaiah 55:7*

# Recommend Worship Song:

# *Mistakes* by Influence & Melody Noel

# How do you feel? Journal your thoughts below.

_____

_____

_____

_____

_____

# Day 6

Inhale God's Will

Exhale All Doubt, Worries, and Fears

God wants and knows what's best for you. We do not know what the future holds but we know that God will be there. In Matthew 6:25–27, Jesus says, "Therefore I tell you, do not worry about your life, what you will eat or drink; or about your body, what you will wear. Is not life more than food and the body more than clothes? Look at the birds of the air; they do not sow or reap or store away in barns, and yet your heavenly Father feeds them. Are you not much more valuable than they? Can any one of you by worrying add a single hour to your life?"

Worrying adds years to our lives; we get stressed out by worries and fears. We should stop worrying and trust God.

# Recommended Scripture Readings:

*Isaiah 40:28-31*

*Jeremiah 29:11-13*

*1 John 4:18*

*Luke 12:22-23*

Recommended Worship Song:

*While I'm Waiting* by Travis Greene

# How do you feel? Journal your thoughts below.

_____

_____

_____

_____

_____

# Day 7

## Conclusion and Prayer

You made it! I pray that you learned something about yourself and God. I hope these past six days that you have let some things go and that you are now feeling free and delivered. Just remember, with God anything is possible. Sometimes, we just have to inhale and exhale and take time to focus and spend time with our Heavenly Father. I hope you enjoyed this journey. May God bless you and keep you. "Now to him who is able to do far more abundantly than all that we ask or think, according to the power at work within us, to him be glory in the church and in Christ Jesus throughout all generations, forever and ever. Amen." (Ephesians 3:20–21)

Sincerely,

Tiffany C. Fuller

# How do you feel? Journal your final thoughts below.

_____

_____

_____

_____

_____

Inhale God's love,
exhale hate

Inhale God's peace,
exhale all anxiety

Inhale God's joy,
exhale unhappiness

Inhale God's forgiveness,
exhale past mistakes

Inhale God's will,
exhale all doubts,
worry and fears

To purchase different items with this poem, please go to the following websites:

https://society6.com/tiff1983

https://fineartamerica.com/profiles/2-tiffany-fuller